Name

Address

Blank Classic

Classic Composition Notebook
(*Red*)
97 numbered pages - 100 total pages
Large 8.5 X 11

Design © 2021 Blank Classic

Blank Classic

Mailing address:
Blank Classic
PO BOX 4608
Main Station Terminal
349 West Georgia Street
Vancouver, BC
Canada, V6B 4A1

Cover design by: Lauren Dick
Interior design by: Lauren Dick

ISBN: 978-1-77476-223-3

FIRST EDITION / FIRST PRINTING

CPSIA information can be obtained
at www.ICGtesting.com
Printed in the USA
LVHW021309130722
723388LV00007B/308

9 781774 762233